Desires of the Heart

Desires of the Heart

A GUIDE TO FINDING YOUR FAITH

DARREN CUSHMAN WOOD

North United Methodist Church • Indianapolis, IN

ISBN 978-1-7327761-3-5 (epub)

ISBN 978-1-7327761-4-2 (paperback)

The cover art comes from a small portion of one of the many beautiful banners throughout North United Methodist Church created by the late Doris Douglas, a long-time member, and other artists.

Contents

Introduction: "Everybody's Got a Hungry Heart"

Whether you are young or old, male or female, rich or poor, we share the same basic desires. Bruce Springsteen said it best:

"Everybody needs a place to rest
Everybody wants to have a home
Don't make no difference what nobody says
Ain't nobody likes to be alone
Everybody's got a hungry heart
Lay down your money and you play your part
Everybody's got a hungry heart.[1]"

St. Augustine would agree. Seventeen hundred years earlier he had a similar perspective on life. What drives us is desire, and at the core of all our desires is our fundamental need for God: "You have made us for yourself, and our heart is restless until it rests in you." Created in the image of God, we long for God to fulfill us and give order to all our wants and needs.

And yet, our hungry hearts eat themselves up. This divine longing is misdirected toward other things that can never satisfy us. But even in these desires is a reflection (to be sure, distorted) of our deeper desire for life in God.

Ironically, when we focus our desire on God, we discover that God fulfills all our desires. All people need the basics: peace, affirmation, purpose, legacy, and companionship. Those basic needs are met when we seek God first.

The central theme of this study is summarized in Psalm 37:4: **"Take delight in the Lord and God will give you the desires of your heart."**

Each session concludes with a prayer exercise on this psalm that will help you focus on the theme for the week and focus your desires with God at the center of your life.

Each week we will explore one of the five basic desires and the way God fulfilled them in the lives of key people in the Old Testament. We can relate to the struggles of David, Joseph, Joshua, Jeremiah, Ruth and Naomi because our needs are timeless, and God is eternal. By reflecting on their stories we can get in touch with our needs. We can learn how to trust in God to give us the desires of our hearts.

Whether you are doing this with a small group or on your own, this study guide is designed to help kindle your passion for God. Each session features reflection questions to aid your personal introspection and to guide your conversations. Each week includes a spiritual exercise based on Psalm 37:4 that you can use every day. Use the weekly hymns for centering yourself in God's presence as you begin each session.

Reader beware: This study will challenge you to take a deeper look at what pushes your buttons. Over the next several weeks listen closely to your heart and do not attempt to arrive at a quick explanation about how you feel. Beware of religiosity. Sometimes we repress our true feelings with religious jargon and try to squeeze the messiness of our feeling into prefabricated spiritual explanations. All God requires is our honesty. If we are willing to let God's Spirit lead us through this process, we will develop a more authentic faith.

IDEAS FOR USING THE CENTERING SONGS

Music is a wonderful way to prepare our hearts and minds for receiving God's word. Each session includes a hymn to begin your personal reflections and small-group conversations. Some of them are well known and a few may be new to you. Here are some ways you can use them:

- Sing them!
- Read them in a round with a different person reading each verse. If there is a refrain, read it in unison.
- After reading each verse, pause for silent prayer.
- Learn the backstory about the song and its composer.

[1] *The River,* Columbia, 1980.

1. Our Desire for Peace

Move over "Game of Thrones," because 1 Samuel 23 begins like a movie. The leading man is on the run, but from whom or what we do not know.

Next there is a flashback so we can learn what has created his desperate fate. The flashback begins in chapter 18 when Jonathan, the son of King Saul, made a covenant with David, who had been put in charge of Saul's troops. Saul's jealousy was inflamed by David's music and popularity, and so he tried to get David killed in battle against their archenemies, the Philistines. Saul promised to give his daughter, Michal, in marriage to David if he would bring back the foreskin of a hundred Philistines as a bride price. To his surprise, David did it and his popularity grew.

Next, Saul plotted to assassinate David, but Michal helped him escape by lowering him down through a window. Later, Jonathan helped David avoid another attempt to trap him. After this, David never returned to Jerusalem, but was on the run with a small band of dissident warriors, outfoxing Saul while fighting the Philistines.

By chapter 23 Saul thinks he has David trapped in the fortress town of Keilah, which David had liberated from the Philistines. But God warned David to retreat into the hills of Ziph before Saul's troops could arrive. Eventually the conflict between David and Saul died down after David caught Saul in a vulnerable spot but refused to kill him (see I Samuel 24). But in this week's reading, Saul still had the upper hand.

Do you remember when your problems were in hot pursuit of you and it felt like they would never end? We long for security and peace of mind. Over time we become weary and react in self-defeating ways if we do not have the assurance of God's protection.

Like the old hymn, we need to learn how to say, "Whatever my lot, thou has taught me to say, it is well, it is well with my soul."

David's story illustrates how God works behind the scenes to protect and guide us through life's struggles. In this session we learn how to look for and trust in God's providential care.

CENTERING SONG: "Stand By Me" by Charles Albert Tindley

When the storms of life are raging,
stand by me (stand by me);
when the storms of life are raging,
stand by me (stand by me).
When the world is tossing me
like a ship upon the sea,
thou who rulest wind and water,
stand by me (stand by me).

In the midst of tribulation,
stand by me (stand by me);
in the midst of tribulation,
stand by me (stand by me).
When the hosts of hell assail,
and my strength begins to fail,
thou who never lost a battle,
stand by me (stand by me).

In the midst of faults and failures,
stand by me (stand by me);
in the midst of faults and failures,
stand by me (stand by me).
When I do the best I can,
and my friends misunderstand,
thou who knowest all about me,
stand by me (stand by me).

In the midst of persecution,
stand by me (stand by me);
in the midst of persecution,
stand by me (stand by me).
When my foes in battle array
undertake to stop my way,
thou who savèd Paul and Silas,
stand by me (stand by me).

When I'm growing old and feeble,
stand by me (stand by me);
when I'm growing old and feeble,
stand by me (stand by me).
when my life becomes a burden,
and I'm nearing chilly Jordan,

O thou "Lily of the Valley,"
stand by me (stand by me).

READING

I Samuel 23:15-29

15David was in the wilderness of Ziph at Horesh when he
learned that Saul had come out to seek his life. 16Saul's son,
Jonathan, set out and came to David at Horesh; there he
strengthened his hand through the Lord. 17He said to him, 'Do
not be afraid; for the hand of my father Saul shall not find
you; you shall be king over Israel, and I shall be second to
you; my father Saul also knows that this is so.' 18Then the two
of them made a covenant before the Lord; David remained at
Horesh, and Jonathan went home. 19Then some Ziphites went
up to Saul at Gibeah and said, 'David is hiding among us in the
strongholds of Horesh, on the hill of Hachilah, which is south
of Jeshimon. 20Now, O king, whenever you wish to come down,
do so; and our part will be to surrender him into the king's
hand.' 21Saul said, 'May you be blessed by the Lord for show-
ing me compassion! 22Go and make sure once more; find out
exactly where he is, and who has seen him there; for I am told
that he is very cunning. 23Look around and learn all the hiding
places where he lurks, and come back to me with sure information. Then I will go with you; and if he is in the land, I will
search him out among all the thousands of Judah.' 24So they set
out and went to Ziph ahead of Saul. David and his men were
in the wilderness of Maon, in the Arabah to the south of Jeshimon. 25Saul and his men went to search for him. When David
was told, he went down to the rock and stayed in the wilderness of Maon. When Saul heard that, he pursued David into

the wilderness of Maon. 26Saul went on one side of the mountain, and David and his men on the other side of the mountain. David was hurrying to get away from Saul, while Saul and his men were closing in on David and his men to capture them. 27Then a messenger came to Saul, saying, 'Hurry and come; for the Philistines have made a raid on the land.' 28So Saul stopped pursuing David, and went against the Philistines; therefore that place was called the Rock of Escape. 29David then went up from there, and lived in the strongholds of Engedi.

EXPLORING THE STORY

What role does Jonathan play in this story?

Compare this story with other events in Jonathan and David's relationship (see I Samuel 18:1-5; 19:1-7; 0:1-42).

What is ironic about Saul's words in v. 21 when compared with I Samuel 18:12?

What caused Saul to stop pursuing David so that he could escape?

EXPLORING OUR STORIES

Right now, how would you rate your level of peace, with one being "completely at peace with my situation" to five being "My problems are in hot pursuit!"

Think of a crisis you faced in the past:

- Who or what was Saul to you? Who or what were the Ziphites that made the crisis worse?

- How did it get resolved? (Did it?)
- As you look back at that crisis, what do you think God was doing at that time in your life?

Check any of the following ways God has given you peace of mind:

___a scripture passage

___a song

___words of another person

___a change of circumstances

___a needed resource

Is God's peace a state of mind or a set of circumstances? Or both?

God used Jonathan to reassure and direct David to safety. Who has been your Jonathan? How did they help you see your present circumstances and/or future prospects differently?

WEEKLY PRAYER EXERCISE WITH PSALM 37:4

"Take delight in the Lord
and God will give you the desires of your heart."

Begin by slowing down your breathing with several long, slow breaths. Then begin a "breath prayer" by thinking or saying quietly as you inhale, "Take delight in the Lord." Then exhale slowly, thinking or saying quietly, "and God will give you the desire of your heart."

Repeat this pattern of inhaling and exhaling for several minutes. Do this breath prayer once a day for one week.

2. Our Desire for Affirmation

Joseph was born into a dysfunctional family system which would make anyone doubt themselves. His father, Jacob, put the "fun" in dysfunctional. His mother, Rachel, was unable to get pregnant, so Jacob fathered two sons with her servant, Bilhah. He did the same thing with his other wife, (Rachel's sister) Leah, and had two more sons with her servant, Zilpah. Eventually Leah gave birth to six more sons. Finally, Rachel was the last to conceive his two youngest boys: Joseph and Benjamin. Two wives, two concubines, and 12 sons in all. No wonder there was competition and turmoil in the house of Israel.

Joseph needed God's affirmation to overcome the brokenness of his family and the challenges of his future. His twofold vision of God's assurance in this week's reading is immediately followed by a series of life-threatening situations. His brothers attacked him and left him for wild animals to kill. His brother Judah sold him to a caravan of Ishmaelites who took him down to Egypt, where he was sold as a house slave to

Potiphar. Potiphar's wife tried to seduce him, and when Joseph resisted, she concocted charges against him that landed him in jail.

Through it all God was working behind the scenes to make his dreams come true. Joseph's talent for dream interpretation opened a door of opportunity for him. While he was in prison, the king's cupbearer and baker were incarcerated, and they needed Joseph's help interpreting their dreams. Years later, after the cupbearer had been released, he recommended that the king tap Joseph for some needed dream work. His interpretations helped the king avoid a disastrous famine and he appointed Joseph governor over his domestic policies. This put Joseph in a key position when his brothers came south to Egypt looking for famine relief.

By the end of the story his original dreams had come true. His brothers had to bow to him. Those boyhood dreams gave him the affirmation he needed to navigate this long, winding journey.

God gives us assurance so that we can navigate the twists and turns of our lives. Paul says, "There is therefore now no condemnation in Jesus Christ....For all who are led by the Spirit of God are children of God" (Romans 8:1, 14). God's unconditional love in Jesus Christ gives us the confidence we need to persevere. When others question and doubt us, God's affirmation remains rock solid. This week we will explore Joseph's story and listen for the Spirit's affirmation for our lives.

CENTERING SONG: "Blessed Assurance" by Fanny Crosby

Blessed assurance, Jesus is mine!
O what a foretaste of glory divine!

Heir of salvation, purchase of God,
born of his Spirit, washed in his blood.

Refrain:
This is my story, this is my song,
praising my Savior all the day long;
this is my story, this is my song,
praising my Savior, all the day long.

Perfect submission, perfect delight,
visions of rapture now burst on my sight;
angels descending bring from above
echoes of mercy, whispers of love.
(Refrain)

Perfect submission, all is at rest;
I in my Savior am happy and blest,
watching and waiting, looking above,
filled with his goodness, lost in his love.
(Refrain)

READING

Genesis 37:2-11

2This is the story of the family of Jacob. Joseph, being 17 years
old, was shepherding the flock with his brothers; he was a
helper to the sons of Bilhah and Zilpah, his father's wives;
and Joseph brought a bad report of them to their father. 3Now
Israel loved Joseph more than any other of his children, because
he was the son of his old age; and he had made him a long
robe with sleeves. 4But when his brothers saw that their father
loved him more than all his brothers, they hated him, and could

not speak peaceably to him. [5]Once Joseph had a dream, and when he told it to his brothers, they hated him even more. [6]He said to them, 'Listen to this dream that I dreamed. [7]There we were, binding sheaves in the field. Suddenly my sheaf rose and stood upright; then your sheaves gathered around it, and bowed down to my sheaf.' [8]His brothers said to him, 'Are you indeed to reign over us? Are you indeed to have dominion over us?' So they hated him even more because of his dreams and his words. [9]He had another dream, and told it to his brothers, saying, 'Look, I have had another dream: the sun, the moon, and 11 stars were bowing down to me.' [10]But when he told it to his father and to his brothers, his father rebuked him, and said to him, 'What kind of dream is this that you have had? Shall we indeed come, I and your mother and your brothers, and bow to the ground before you?' [11]So his brothers were jealous of him, but his father kept the matter in mind.

EXPLORING THE STORY

What do we learn about the family dynamics?

What are your impressions of Joseph and his dreams? Was this youthful arrogance or godly confidence?

How might these dreams have given Joseph courage to face future trials and to handle future success?

EXPLORING OUR STORIES

What has shaken your confidence?

Have you ever been criticized for doing the right thing? Were you aware of God's presence at that time?

How has God given you reassurance and affirmation (choose as many as apply):

___ a special scripture passage
___ words of others
___ a dream or vision
___ an award, promotion, or other form of recognition
___ an unusual experience
___ a feeling of calm assurance
___ a song

Timeline of Your Blessed Assurance:

Make a timeline of the major events in your life. Above the line make a checkmark for all the good things and an X for all the hard times. Then, below the line put one of the following letters to indicate what God was doing in your life: directing (D), correcting (C), protecting (P), sustaining (S), and/or affirming (A).

How can we distinguish between human arrogance and divine affirmation?

When have you seen someone seeking the wrong kind of affirmation?

WEEKLY PRAYER EXERCISE WITH PSALM 37:4

"Take delight in the Lord and God will give you the desires of your heart."

Over the next five days, focus on each one of your five senses:

- Day 1: seeing
- Day 2: hearing
- Day 3: tasting
- Day 4: touching
- Day 5: smelling

Focus on the sense assigned to each day and let your senses help you become aware of God's delight. For example, on day five become conscious of the things you like to smell.

Begin and end each day by reciting Psalm 37:4, and throughout the day as you think about and experience the delights of your senses, consider how you are experiencing God through that particular sense.

At each day's end, give God thanks for those divine encounters.

3. Our Desire for Purpose

In 2002 Rick Warren published "The Purpose Driven Life." This devotional book outlines a 40-day program for discerning God's calling. In the first five years, Zondervan sold over 30 million copies. The book's popularity reflects a basic human desire for purpose and meaning. Merely existing is never enough; we long for a sense of direction from a higher power and a purpose greater than ourselves whom we can serve.

God gave Joshua clear direction for his future, but Joshua was unsure he was up for the task. Moses, his mentor and leader, had died before they reached Canaan. Now God was passing on Moses' mantle to Joshua to lead them into the promised land.

Why Joshua? He had been loyal when everyone else had worshipped the golden calf. He and Caleb were the only scouts that had reported back to Moses that the Israelites could indeed be victorious if they entered Canaan. Yet Joshua had always been a lieutenant, never the general. Now God was calling him to a bigger mission.

In this session we will examine the ways God calls us. Like Joshua, we will confront our questions and reservations, and we will discover how God is equipping us for a purpose greater than ourselves.

CENTERING SONG: "We Are Called" by David Haas

Come! Live in the light!
Shine with the joy and the love of the Lord!
We are called to be light for the kingdom,
to live in the freedom of the city of God!

Refrain:
We are called to act with justice,
we are called to love tenderly,
we are called to serve one another,
to walk humbly with God.

Come! Open your heart!
Show your mercy to all those in fear!
We are called to be hope for the hopeless
so all hatred and blindness will be no more!
(Refrain)

Sing! Sing a new song!
Sing of that great day when all will be one!
God will reign, and we'll walk with each other
as sisters and brothers united in love!
(Refrain)

READING

Joshua 1:1-9

[1]After the death of Moses, the servant of the Lord, the Lord spoke to Joshua, son of Nun, Moses' assistant, saying, [2]'My servant Moses is dead. Now proceed to cross the Jordan, you and all his people, into the land that I am giving to them, to the Israelites. [3]Every place that the sole of your foot will tread upon I have given to you, as I promised to Moses. [4]From the wilderness and Lebanon as far as the great river, the river Euphrates, all the land of the Hittites, to the Great Sea in the west shall be your territory. [5]No one shall be able to stand against you all the days of your life. As I was with Moses, so I will be with you; I will not fail you or forsake you. [6]Be strong and courageous; for you shall put this people in possession of the land that I swore to their ancestors to give them. [7]Only be strong and very courageous, being careful to act in accordance with all the law that my servant Moses commanded you; do not turn from it to the right hand or to the left, so that you may be successful wherever you go. [8]This book of the law shall not depart out of your mouth; you shall meditate on it day and night, so that you may be careful to act in accordance with all that is written in it. For then you shall make your way prosperous, and then you shall be successful. [9]I hereby command you: 'Be strong and courageous; do not be frightened or dismayed, for the Lord your God is with you wherever you go.'

EXPLORING THE STORY

What promise is given to Joshua and how many times is it given (v. 3-5, 9)?

What role does the past play in giving him confidence to take on this task (v. 6)?

What must Joshua do to be successful (v. 7)?

EXPLORING OUR STORIES

When have you been given a task that you felt inadequate to take on?

As you look back over your life, when have you felt the strongest sense that a particular job or venture was God's will? When have you had the most doubt about God's purpose?

Rank the following in terms of how well they help you discern God's will for your future (one=least helpful; seven=most helpful):

___ conversation with other people
___ listening for the Spirit through worship and song
___ finding confirmation in a scripture passage
___ change of circumstances and new opportunities opening up
___ long walks and quiet meditation
___ making a list of all your options and outlining the pros and cons
___ other:

What do you think is God's direction for your life right now? How has God been preparing you?

What role does obedience to God play in determining whether or not something is God's will?

What happens to us when we do not pursue our callings? What prevents us from pursuing it?

WEEKLY PRAYER EXERCISE WITH PSALM 37:4

"Take delight in the Lord and God will give you the desires of your heart."

Step 1: Say silently several times: "Take delight in the Lord" and center your thoughts on God, meditating on the attributes of God. What is the one characteristic of God that comes to the forefront of your thinking?

Step 2: Then, say silently several times: "and God will give me the desires of my heart." Ask yourself: "What do I desire over and over again?" Then ask yourself: "Do these desires express some deeper needs I have?"

Step 3: Finally, using the characteristic identified in Step 1 as a name for God, offer the following prayer: "[your name for God], I surrender my desires to you." For example, if the characteristic is divine power, you might pray: "Strong God, I surrender my desires to you."

4. Our Desire for a Legacy

A few years ago, my wife, Ginny, and I finalized our wills. They include standard language about the inheritance of personal property, such as our automobiles. Our daughters got a good laugh when we shared that one of them would inherit "Old Chamey." That was the name they gave our 1999 Pontiac Montana because its color was champagne. The Montana may have been like any number of alcoholic beverages, but champagne was not one of them. So, no one was disappointed when one of the girls totaled Old Chamey late one night, which improved their inheritance with a new car.

All of us have a need to leave a legacy, even if it is in chrome and rubber. Perhaps it has something to do with our desire for immortality, or maybe it is the sense that we are a part of something larger than ourselves. From the beginning of time humans have sought to leave their mark in stone, wood, and paper for future generations to remember that they were here.

God fulfills this desire by inviting us to participate in God's hope. We contribute to God's future plans through our acts of mercy, justice, and peace. The legacy we leave is an act of faith, trusting that God will bring to completion what we have started long after we are gone.

It was an outrageous act of faith for Jeremiah to leave his legacy in the land. This session's reading is a real estate deal. There could not have been a worse time to invest in property. Jerusalem was under siege by the Babylonians and Jeremiah was in prison in the capital city. They would be sacked and deported shortly. A few miles away was his hometown of Anathoth, the ancient home of priests. By law, he had the first rights to the homestead, but why would he want it, given the dire political situation? As a prophet who had foretold the invasion and impending deportation, Jeremiah knew the score. And yet God wanted him to buy it as his legacy.

As you explore Jeremiah's legacy, listen for God's opportunities for your own legacy.

CENTERING SONG: "The Gift of Love" by Hal Hopson

Though I may speak with bravest fire,
and have the gift to all inspire,
and have not love, my words are vain,
as sounding brass, and hopeless gain.

Though I may give all I possess,
and striving so my love profess,
but not be given by love within,
the profit soon turns strangely thin.

Come, Spirit, come, our hearts control,
our spirits long to be made whole.

Let inward love guide every deed;
by this we worship, and are freed.

READING

Jeremiah 32:6-19

[6]Jeremiah said, “The word of the Lord came to me: [7]Hanamel, son of your uncle, Shallum, is going to come to you and say, ‘Buy my field that is at Anathoth, for the right of redemption by purchase is yours.’ “[8]Then my cousin Hanamel came to me in the court of the guard, in accordance with the word of the Lord, and said to me, ‘Buy my field that is at Anathoth in the land of Benjamin, for the right of possession and redemption is yours; buy it for yourself.’ Then I knew that this was the word of the Lord. [9]And I bought the field at Anathoth from my cousin Hanamel, and weighed out the money to him, 17 shekels of silver. [10]I signed the deed, sealed it, got witnesses, and weighed the money on scales. [11]Then I took the sealed deed of purchase, containing the terms and conditions, and the open copy; [12]and I gave the deed of purchase to Baruch, son of Neriah, son of Mahseiah, in the presence of my cousin Hanamel, in the presence of the witnesses who signed the deed of purchase, and in the presence of all the Judeans who were sitting in the court of the guard. [13]In their presence I charged Baruch, saying, [14]“Thus says the Lord of hosts, the God of Israel: Take these deeds, both this sealed deed of purchase and this open deed, and put them in an earthenware jar, in order that they may last for a long time.’ [15]For thus says the Lord of hosts, the God of Israel: Houses and fields and vineyards shall again be bought in this land. [16]After I had given the deed of purchase to Baruch, son of Neriah, I prayed to the Lord, saying: [17]‘Ah, Lord God!

It is you who made the heavens and the earth by your great power and by your outstretched arm! Nothing is too hard for
you. 18You show steadfast love to the thousandth generation, but repay the guilt of parents into the laps of their children after them, O great and mighty God, whose name is the Lord
of hosts, 19great in counsel and mighty in deed; whose eyes are open to all the ways of mortals, rewarding all according to their ways and according to the fruit of their doings.'

EXPLORING THE STORY

What does the purchase of land symbolize about God's hope?

What does it tell us about Jeremiah's faith? What doubts do you think he had?

Is his prayer a celebration of or a resignation to God's will (v. 17-25)?

EXPLORING OUR STORIES

Is there one thing you would hope your family and friends would keep in remembrance of you?

Is there one thing you hope they get rid of?

How have you been impacted by someone's legacy?

What comfort is there in a long-term assurance when you are facing an immediate crisis?

What role does prayer play in your decision making about the future?

God calls us to make an investment right now that will become our legacy of faith. Check any of the following types of "investments" you feel you need to make:

___a financial gift
___sharing your experience and skills with another person
___giving your time to an organization
___affirming someone
___other:

What challenges do we face in leaving a faithful legacy?

WEEKLY PRAYER EXERCISE WITH PSALM 37:4

"Take delight in the Lord and God will give you the desires of your heart."

Begin by reading Psalm 37:4 as an opening prayer, inviting God to guide your thinking.

Part 1: Review your spending on all nonessential things over the past month. How do you define what is nonessential? What does this say about what you take delight in?

Part 2: Review all your giving, investing, and savings. What does this say about the desires of your heart?

End your time of meditation by reading Psalm 37:4 as a prayer of dedication.

5. Our Desire for Companionship

My great-grandmother, Lola Brown, lived across the field and down the road. She shared a plot of land with her sister-in-law, Lula Brown. They lived beside each other for decades after their husbands (brothers Walter and Wesley) passed away. Their tiny houses were divided by a pea-gravel driveway and a thick row of peonies.

"Lolo" and "Luli," as we kids knew them, spent their days tending their truck patch garden. At night, when Luli heard strange noises scratching at her window (she claimed they were demons), Lolo would walk over and reassure her that all was safe.

Bruce Springsteen is right: "Don't make no difference what nobody says/ain't nobody likes to be alone/everybody's got a hungry heart."

In this session we will explore the universal need for companionship. We are not solitary creatures. Created in the image of the Triune God, we are spiritually wired to be in relationships for the flourishing of human life. Whether it is a spouse, a cousin, a neighbor, a coworker or a friend, our hearts are hungry for companionship. God fulfills that desire by bringing people and pets into our lives who will affirm and challenge us to become what God has made us to be.

The book of Ruth begins with a crisis that threatens human flourishing. Famine is in the land of Moab. Years earlier Elimelech and Naomi had moved to Moab from their hometown of Bethlehem. Their two sons had married Moabite girls, Orpah and Ruth. Ten years later famine hit and the men died. Three widows were left destitute in a patriarchal culture and collapsing economy.

When Naomi decided to return to her hometown, her daughters-in-law were supposed to seek help from their Moabite extended families. Watch closely for what Ruth decided to do, because it is one of the most profound acts of faith in the Bible.

CENTERING SONG: "Draw Us in the Spirit's Tether" by Percy Dearmer

Draw us in the Spirit's tether,
for when humbly in thy name,
two or three are met together,
thou art in the midst of them.
Alleluia! Alleluia!
Touch we now thy garment's hem.

As disciples used to gather
in the name of Christ to sup,
then with thanks to God the Father,
break the bread and bless the cup:

Alleluia! Alleluia!
So now bind our friendship up.

All our meals and all our living
make as sacraments of thee,
that by caring, helping, giving,
we may true disciples be.
Alleluia! Alleluia!
We will serve thee faithfully.

READING

Ruth 1:6-18

6Then she started to return with her daughters-in-law from the country of Moab, for she had heard in the country of Moab that the Lord had had consideration for his people and given them food. 7So she set out from the place where she had been living, she and her two daughters-in-law, and they went on their way to go back to the land of Judah. 8But Naomi said to her two daughters-in-law, 'Go back each of you to your mother's house. May the Lord deal kindly with you, as you have dealt with the dead and with me. 9The Lord grant that you may find security, each of you in the house of your husband.' Then she kissed them, and they wept aloud. 10They said to her, 'No, we will return with you to your people.' 11But Naomi said, 'Turn back, my daughters, why will you go with me? Do I still have sons in my womb that they may become your husbands? 12Turn back, my daughters, go your way, for I am too old to have a husband. Even if I thought there was hope for me, even if I should have a husband tonight and bear sons, 13would you then wait until they were grown? Would you then refrain from marrying? No, my daughters, it has been far more bitter for me than for you, because the hand of the Lord has turned against me.' [14]Then they wept aloud again. Orpah kissed her mother-in-law, but Ruth clung to her. [15]So she said, 'See, your sister-in-law has gone back to her people and to her gods; return after your sister-in-law.' [16]But Ruth said, 'Do not press me to leave you or to turn back from following you! Where you go, I will go; where you lodge, I will lodge; your people shall be my people, and your God my God. [17]Where you die, I will die – there will I be buried. May the Lord do thus and so to me, and more as well, if even death parts me from you!' [18]When Naomi saw that she was determined to go with her, she said no more to her.

EXPLORING THE STORY

Why does Naomi tell Orpah and Ruth to turn back?

How is Ruth's decision an act of faith?

Compare it with Abram's act of faith in Genesis 12:1-9. How is her decision a more profound act of faith than Abram's?

Why do you think Naomi was silent at the end of the story (v. 18)?

Read the entire book of Ruth. How does God respond to Ruth's fidelity to Naomi?

EXPLORING OUR STORIES

When faced with a problem, is your tendency to share it with others or to keep it to yourself?

Think of a crisis you faced and you were supported by another person. What did they do that was helpful (check as many as apply)?

___a quiet presence
___gave good advice
___allowed you to complain and share your feelings
___advocated for you
___did something concrete that was helpful
___other:

What risks do we take in being a companion (Ruth) and in receiving companionship (Naomi)?

There were religious and ethnic conflicts between Israelites and Moabites (see Genesis 19:30-38; Numbers 25:1-3). When have religious or ethnic differences complicated your relationships? When have you been blessed by a diversity of friends?

Has God ever blessed you with the companionship of another creature?

WEEKLY PRAYER EXERCISE WITH PSALM 37:4

"Take delight in the Lord and God will give you the desires of your heart."

Pray for a different person each day of the week using Psalm 37:4 as the form of intercessory prayer: "May [name] take delight in you, Lord, and may you fulfill the desires of his/her heart."

About the Author

Darren Cushman Wood is the senior pastor of North United Methodist Church in Indianapolis, Indiana. He has served small and large, rural and urban United Methodist churches for over 30 years. He is a graduate of the University of Evansville and Union Theological Seminary.

He is the author of two books, hymns, and numerous articles. He is an adjunct professor of labor studies at Indiana University. He is married to Ginny and as of this writing they have three adult children and one grandchild.

www.ingramcontent.com/pod-product-compliance
Lightning Source LLC
LaVergne TN
LVHW020313110826
845148LV00017BA/2650
* 9 7 8 1 7 3 2 7 7 6 1 4 2 *